ny maniacal author
amility anchor
amanitarian clay hut
halation aura
horal unanimity
ti-haircut anomaly
ctual Haitian hymn
hatty malaria union
atch your Italian human
aniacal Torah unity
ail uncouth martian
ot hairy nautical human
ythic national aura
uman utility anchor
nnual Haiti youth march
aunt touchy animal hair
aturation chain
lt hairy continuum
utuality chain
horal humanity unit
aul a humanity chariot
uman Titanic hourly
lian canary-mouth
arity mountain
nhurt anatomical
util mahayana choir
unch martini youth
nitarian halo
anical hour hath unity
ctual anatomy chain
ational haircut
ul martian youth chain

Hail marathon acuity
Tute
Ch
Lau
Un
Uni
Unl
Hi, a..., ... human author
Unhurt intimacy halo

SEA PEACH
(Halocynthia auranthium)

Tiny maniacal author
Humility anchor
Humanitarian clay hut
Inhalation aura
Choral unanimity
Anti-haircut anomaly
Actual Haitian hymn
Chatty malaria union
Hatch your Italian human
Maniacal Torah unity
Hail uncouth martian
Hot hairy nautical human
Mythic national aura
Human utility anchor
Annual Haiti youth march
Haunt touchy animal hair
Maturation chain

Mutuality chain

MW01598225

Untu manayana choir
Launch martini youth
Unitarian halo
Manical hour hath unity
Ritual anatomy chain
National haircut
Haul martian youth chain
Our hyacinth animal
Hail marathon acuity
Tutorial human chain
Choral humanity unit
Launch humanity aorta
Uncouth hairy animal hat
Unitary animal hath ouch
Unhurt holy Ithaca mania
Hi, analytic human author!
Unhurt intimacy halo
Tiny maniacal author
Humility anchor
Humanitarian clay hut
Inhalation aura
Choral unanimity
Anti-haircut anomaly
Actual Haitian hymn
Chatty malaria union

Tiny maniacal author
Humility anchor
Humanitarian clay hut
Inhalation aura
Choral unanimity
Anti-haircut anomaly
Actual Haitian hymn
Chatty malaria union
Hatch your Italian human
Maniacal Torah unity
Hail uncouth martian
Hot hairy nautical human
Mythic national aura
Human utility anchor
Annual Haiti youth march
Haunt touchy animal hair
Maturation chain
Halt hairy continuum
Mutuality chain
Choral humanity unit
Haul a humanity chariot
Human Titanic hourly
Italian canary-mouth
Clarity mountain
Unhurt anatomical
Until mahayana choir
Launch martini youth
Unitarian halo
Manical hour hath unity
Ritual anatomy chain
National haircut
Haul martian youth chain

Hail marathon acuity
Tutorial human chain
Choral humanity unit
Launch humanity aorta
Uncouth hairy animal hat
Unitary animal hath ouch
Unhurt holy Ithaca mania
Hi, analytic human author!
Unhurt intimacy halo
Tiny maniacal author
Humility anchor
Humanitarian clay hut
Inhalation aura
Choral unanimity
Anti-haircut anomaly
Actual Haitian hymn
Chatty malaria union
Hatch your Italian human
Maniacal Torah unity
Hail uncouth martian
Hot hairy nautical human
Mythic national aura
Human utility anchor
Annual Haiti youth march
Haunt touchy animal hair
Maturation chain
Halt hairy continuum
Mutuality chain
Choral humanity unit
Haul a humanity chariot
Human Titanic hourly
Italian canary-mouth

Unhurt anatomical
Until mahayana choir
Launch martini youth
Unitarian halo
Manical hour hath unity
Ritual anatomy chain
National haircut
Haul martian youth chain
Our hyacinth animal
Hail marathon acuity
Tutorial human chain
Choral humanity unit
Launch humanity aorta
Uncouth hairy animal hat
Unitary animal hath ouch
Unhurt holy Ithaca mania
Hi, analytic human author!
Unhurt intimacy halo
Tiny maniacal author
Humility anchor
Humanitarian clay hut
Inhalation aura
Choral unanimity
Anti-haircut anomaly
Actual Haitian hymn
Chatty malaria union
Hatch your Italian human
Maniacal Torah unity
Hail uncouth martian
Hot hairy nautical human
Mythic national aura
Human utility anchor

SEA PEACH

(Halocynthia auranthium)

Catherine Kidd
Jack Beetz

Words and voice: Catherine Kidd
Soundscapes on CD mixed, arranged, and produced by Jack Beetz
Book designed and produced by Andy Brown for conundrum press
Executive producer for Wired on Words: Ian Ferrier
First edition of 1000 copies / © 2002

National Library of Canada Cataloguing in Publication

Kidd, Catherine, 1967–
    Sea peach : halocynthia auranthium / Catherine Kidd.

Includes CD, arranged and produced by Jack Beetz.
ISBN 0-9689496-4-9

    1. Prose poems, Canadian (English) I. Beetz, Jack II. Title.

PS8571.I34S42 2002   C811'.6   C2002-903589-9
PR9199.3.K4286S42 2002

Dépot Legal, Bibliothèque nationale du Québec

conundrum press
P.O. Box 55003 CSP Fairmount, Montreal, Quebec, H2T 3E2
conpress@ican.net   http://home.ican.net/~conpress

The Canada Council | Le Conseil des Arts
for the Arts | du Canada

This book and CD were produced with the financial
assistance of the Canada Council for the Arts and the
Department of Canadian Heritage through IPOLC.

1. Downward Facing Dog
Agnes goes home with a man she meets in front of the buffalo pen at the zoo.
This is the very first time she has done this.

2. A Big Fat Hen
They go for a walk, and speak of chickens.
Later, Agnes meets the ghost of her father in the bathroom.

3. The Walking Man
A recurring nightmare about muffled footsteps.

4. Global Warming
The meltdown of Agnes and Noah, and meditations on protozoa.

5. The Tale of the Horse Leech
Written for Agnes on her eleventh birthday.
She finds it in a biscuit tin, years later.

6. Happy the 3-Legged Ghost Hamster
Agnes drags her father's typewriter from the closet and learns how to misspell.

7. Sea Peach
The sea peach is a creature who looks like a heart.

DOWNWARD FACING DOG

Amazing. Like watching a sea turtle laying eggs is amazing. Or like a man escaping from an underwater box where he is chained and hand-cuffed in a straight-jacket is amazing. I thought that something would burst, something would split, thought the water we were made of would rush and merge with the water we were tossed upon, like stripped barks, thrown one against the other in serges and ebbs.

Or really what I thought was that the water mattress would burst open and we'd both be soaked, and I'd arrive back home at my mother's door like a drowned thing, returning from the deep with strands of kelp in my hair. I didn't realize how unlikely this was, any more than I could admit the secret plan of never returning home at all.

He seemed to be wholly large. Just a very large man, the whole ceiling descending. At least in the sense of things seeming very large when seen *very close up*. Like those visual games where they take a close-up photograph of some object or surface, and you're supposed to guess what it is. Assuming you're not accustomed to seeing it from such intimate perspective, which I wasn't. The body of the Buffalo Man was a whole series of these photographs. *Can you guess? Hirsute surface, smooth dome, puckered crease, bony projection, mobile elastic fold.* And my responses, reciprocal:

mobile elastic fold,   *bony projection,*

   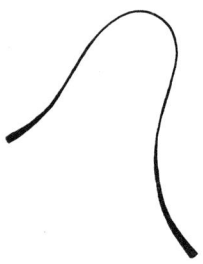

puckered crease, smooth dome, hirsute surface.

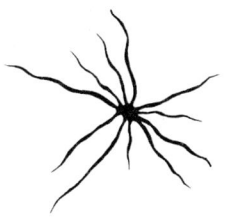

But separately, and above all of this, I sensed another part, suspended above us among the wooden rafters. From this remote perspective we were creature-small, pale and strange, jerking like puppets. From there, I had to wonder who he was. What manner of beast he was, and how I came to be there in the room with him. This suspended part, this imp-in-the-rafters was not hungry from the longing to be touched, like the parts below. This impish part watched, and laughed, and thought *What fools, these mortals, why would they? why do they? Tomorrow, conclusions will be drawn up. Objectives will be proven true or false, just as they have a thousand thousand times before. And then what is to be done with the specimens, once they're splayed open and named, once it is done? What do we do with the bodies?*

I don't try to fake any conclusions. I couldn't have done this anyway, I'd never been in such a position before. I didn't really know what it was supposed to *feel* like on the *inside,* only what it was supposed to *look* like from the *outside.* Women in movies usually said *Yes yes,* while at times I found my voice straining toward *No no,* though I know these things are supposed to mean the opposite.

Then comes a moment like a stroke, when the body is caught, delirium tremens in suspension, then *Does she fall or does she not?* Either one as easy, as impossible as the other. *Don't push me, No, Yes, push me down down and up up out of myself, into myself, into you and you and I disappear entirely.* Another sort of beast entirely, with two of almost everything. Two backs, two mouths, four legs. Narcissistic parasitic epileptic hermaphrodite. Two hearts and two bad livers and two of those oyster-like spaces beneath our two tongues, where pellets of poison may be hidden, or pearls.

Amazing, too, that masks of tragedy and comedy fit together so well on a bed, framed as on a stage. Beatific and low. Febrific and slow. Pelagic libido, catastrophic placebo, conspecific peepshow, geomorphic yo-yo, anthropophagic tic-tac-toe, magic deathblow, protoplasmic echo, tragic curio, sudorific tremolo, soporific airflow. Beatific and low, febrific and slow, pelagic libido, catastrophic placebo, conspecific peepshow, geomorphic yo-yo, anthropophagic tic-tac-toe, magic deathblow, protoplasmic echo, tragic curio, sudorific tremolo, soporific airflow. Beatific and low, febrific and slow, pelagic libido, catastrophic placebo, conspecific peepshow, geomorphic yo-yo, anthropophagic tic-tac-toe, magic deathblow, protoplasmic echo, tragic curio, sudorific tremolo, soporific airflow.

Beatific and low, febrific and slow, pelagic libido,

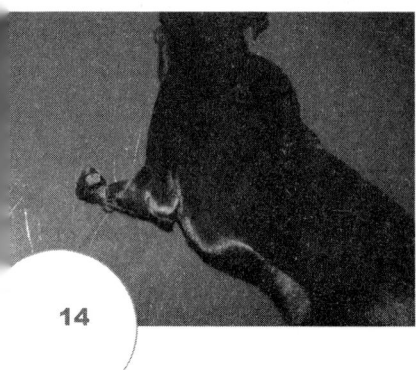

catastrophic placebo, conspecific peepshow, geo-

morphic yo-yo, anthropophagic tic-tac-toe,

magic deathblow, protoplasmic echo,

tragic curio, sudorific tremolo,

soporific airflow...

A BIG FAT HEN

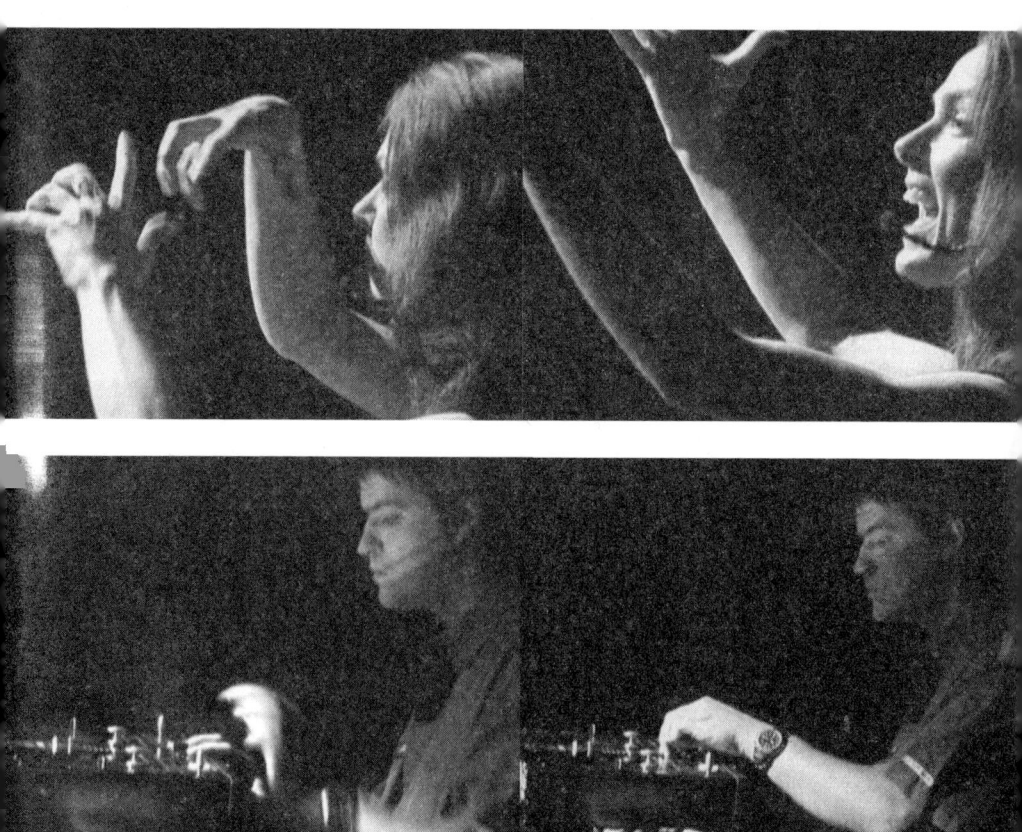

After my Achilles heals, the Buffalo Man and I take walks along Commercial Drive. He wears those molded sandals with rubber-tire soles, and fitted straps, like he could unravel his shoes and repel down a cliff with the parts. I wear canvas shoes from Chinatown.

Buffalo Man and I do not notice the same things when we walk. This is something I notice. I also tend to notice things like cappuccino cups with foam scum still on the rim, and dogs who've run round the pole they're tethered to a few too many times, red leashes getting wound round like a barber shop, with the dog clinging close and whining whiskered like a drunk. The Buffalo Man notices a sticker for a local hardcore band, on a crosswalk breaker, with a picture of a Dr. Suess fox carrying an axe. Then he notices a woman who looks exactly like Tippi Hedren, she just got on that bus, he swears to God. He can't understand how I could have missed her.

Then, in the window of a junk shop, we both notice an old tin sign, bent and rusty with the words *Tattooed Poultry* in black block letters.

For several blocks we talk about what *Tattooed Poultry* might mean. The Buffalo Man thinks it's an advertisement, that you could once have gone to this place and got your hens tattooed, so no other guy could claim they were his hens. Or maybe these people sold exotic hens, and had the whole coop of them tattooed as proof of pedigree.

So then I start talking about what-all misery the hens of the world were subjected to, foot diseases from standing in overcrowded dirty coops, and being made to lay eggs constantly. Poultry fowl being executed with electric probes inserted under their beaks. I must have mentioned the electric probes at least a half dozen times, even a dozen, I couldn't make the image go away no matter how quickly we walked.

You could slow down a bit, you know, says the Buffalo Man.

There's something so personal about beaks, I continue, *so intrinsic to the identity of hens. So much depends on beaks. It's because of beaks that we got to pick out the yellow and orange crayons to colour in pictures of chickens, instead of just red for the wattle and comb. Because most chickens in pictures are left white, for some reason. You felt like you were supposed to leave the body white. Like the White Spot hen.*

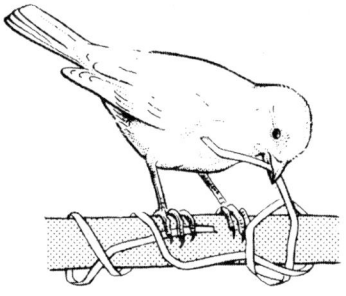

And the colouring books never said boo about electric probes.

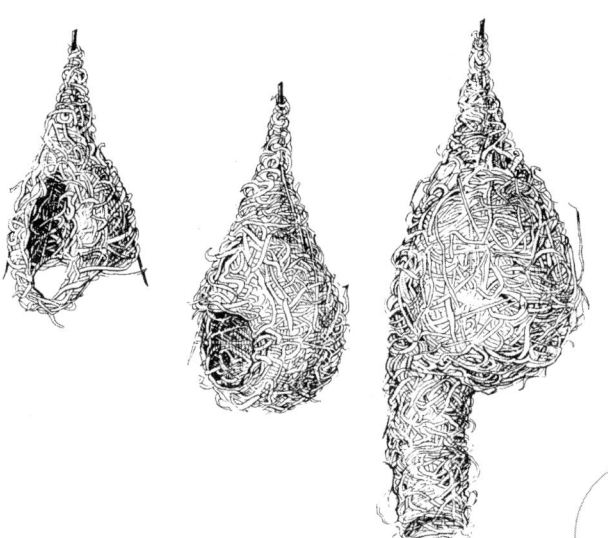

The Buffalo Man cuts in and says he wants me to stop dwelling on electrocuted hens, but I cannot stop dwelling on them until I understand why the image persists. *So much depends* on understanding why an image does not flow away into grey matter, like so many of them do, but gets caught in some mental appendix and inflames the place. Demanding to be extracted, expressed, at least identified. Relative heavens and hells seem to seed in the naming of pictures.

I'd like to get one of those beaded curtains, one of the bamboo ones, I say, when a golden haired woman walks past, fragrant of amber, with sand-soft bead-sounds rustling in her hair, and silver toe-rings. Probably she had beaded curtains as well, and could read a person's palms, with all of her exits entrancing through shimmering sheaves, like a goddess of wheat. And I was a goddess of beaks. A goddess of ungainly mouths, which squeak and squawk and are frequently heard to say nothing. A goddess of shock-mouth hens who don't peck back, electrically pecked in the pecker.

The mouth of a cup, with dried cappuccino scum. Round. Open. Receptive. Silent. I didn't want to emulate these qualities, wholly, but when I saw their expression in objects, the foam on the mouth of a cup, I did feel a tug in my chest like I'd open a robe to receive them.

Later, lying back in the tub, I wash my hair with egg shampoo and dunk my whole head to rinse it. I am tempted to taste it, and do so, but it doesn't taste like eggs at all. While my eyes are still closed, and my ears underwater, I imagine the sound of a drill, and for a moment I am drowning in a dentist chair at Dr. Spector's clinic. My mother is rinsing cherry fluoride from my teeth with a shiny metal water-pistol, another trigger shooting off only cold air. Cold air and water hitting my two front teeth, the two fake ones, and splashing up into my nose. *If the teeth are fake, why can I still feel them? If something is not real, why can you still feel its breath on the back of your neck when you walk home late at night?*

I sit up suddenly in the tub, streaming egg shampoo from hair tendrils, the water tepid and soupy. *Egg drop soup.* By accident of nerves, I drop the cool egg of soap into the tub, and feel around in the suds until I find it. Like an eel it eludes, drawing in eddies my brain again to the place where I am always reaching beneath the surface, toward something unseen and unremembered, into the warmish dampish depth it dwells within. When I bathe, or wash dishes, or pry open the drain with a dinner fork to dig out the carrot-coin which is clogging it, I expect to find memory in such places. *But could not the same naked woman as I am climb up on a rooftop, and catch memory in the flashes of an electrical storm? Could there not be more light involved, and air, and space, and sparks?*

The sound of the drill starts up again, and the bathroom door shimmies on its hinges. The room is tilting sideways perhaps. I hold onto the water fixtures, hot and cold in my hands, as onto a world which is fixed when the mind shimmies. But no, not much of the world is *fixed*. The world is a stray cat who prowls the alleys and sires many, bears many, buries many. Nothing is fixed, but all is in need of fixing. Fixing is the state of desire, it moves and envelopes. A fine fix is what we all are in, we are.

I watch the door, fix eyes. It tips toward me ajar, a crooked jar, then the barbarous face of the Buffalo Man, grinning with a ball cap on backwards. There's a leather strap across his forehead where I might expect to see a spot light, like he's one of those guys in mines who blow holes in walls, breaking through to hidden caverns.

Why'd you take the whole bathroom door off? I ask. Aside from the taxidermy studio, the bathroom had been the only closed space in the Buffalo Man's place. But now, in the empty doorway, he stands on a barstool and hammers two nails above the frame, with the hammer of Thor, a small steel hammer which came attached to the hand of an eighteen-inch action figure. The Buffalo Man uses Thor's hammer to free Thor from his usual hanging-place above the door, before driving home the two new nails. From my seat in the cold bath, all I can see of the Buffalo Man is his hands and his slouchy trousers, his American bison belt buckle, and the unbuttoned belly of his green work shirt. Now that the bathroom door has been removed, I am prickly with a cold draft.

What are you doing, anyway? I ask.

Shush, he says, *it's supposed to be a birthday present. I got it for you today when you were conversing with stray dogs on the Drive, Miss Doolittle.*

Then, from the two new nails, the Buffalo Man hangs a shimmering sheave of bamboo beads. There is the sound of a rain stick as they settle plumb. Once the beads have stilled, I can make out the picture painted on them. There are two elephants, with green foliage all around. They are either walking side by side, or they're mounted on each other, it is difficult to tell. But from certain angles, or if there's too much back-light, the painted elephants disappear entirely, like the purple Two Lions across Burrard Inlet.

Before leaving the bathroom, I catch sight of my face in the steamy mirror. If time continues to co-operate with gravity, I will look exactly like my father in twenty years. Hopefully without the beard. But if a vision fixed *upward* continues to be made impractical by perpetual clouds, or I fail to learn to laugh at things, my brows will continue to knit a low creased awning over my eyes. And I will look exactly like my father, in twenty years, or maybe ten. I know this, not from a very clear memory of my father's face, but something more akin to a haunting in mine. Yet finally, when the mirror speaks, it is with my voice, not his.

Don't go back, Agnes. You are obsessed with going backwards. So you think you're changed, do you? Whose face do you seek when you look into his eyes? The past is a garage sale, Agnes, you pick the things which seem to be valuable, you take them home. And in time comes meaning, like a holy garage sale grail. But remember, you could have picked other things instead.

Walking through the beads makes a sound like hidden rattlesnakes, when I leave the bathroom to join the Buffalo Man in the lighted loft. The painted elephants disperse, they shimmy between sheaves and disappear, reassembling themselves only after the sway and hiss have passed. But looking back a bit later, I see them there again, the pair of mountainous elephants, still shaking slightly.

THE WALKING MAN

The Walking Man had been an object of desire for as long as there was breath, he had simply always been there. Even Darth Vader, my later obsession, was derivative of him. Or Vader was the voice and hands of him, who had no voice, no hands, no form in space (except the sound of his footsteps, which was incessant). But like breath in meditation, his steps were only noticeable when focused upon, and then became all-consuming, unbearable, huge like death. Minute and desolate, like death. And so I only noticed it sometimes, the muffled sound of his footsteps through dead leaves, usually at night, just as I was falling asleep. Even if I buried my head beneath a pillow I couldn't smother the sound, once it had arrested me, it only amplified itself. Like the lover on the Grecian urn, the Walking Man was never to be reached, would never reach me, only pursue me forever walking.

Sometimes the sound would feed upon itself.

Sometimes the sound would feed upon itself, the footsteps of the Walking Man would quicken by the very act of my listening to them. I would break into a sweat and plead with him to stop his steps. But this would only make him walk more quickly, the sound rushing in my ears, quickening my pulse. The warmer I became, the more quickly walked the Walking Man. He excited me. I desired him. I wished that he would come to me and crush me at last, or quit me once and for all, quit his walking once and for all and leave me rest in peace.

I felt compelled to give him form, in my mind's eye. He was tall, and dressed in a black cloak which sloped about his ankles, obscuring his feet, which did not appear to touch the ground at all. It was amazing to me that he could make a sound, he whose feet seemed not to strike the earth, but only struck a barrier of some sort, and broke it clean, creating sound.

It was several years before I realized his true identity. And so I find the first man I desired was nothing but a little girl, *myself*, reading her *own pulse* as a pursuer. A suitor, a man relying on the beating of her dislocated heart to move his steps, just as she relied on his pursuit to stir her pulse. And so the barest sustenance is implicated with desire, to be an object of the Walking Man's desire. To be a little girl who figures her own pulse as exiled, aged, and other.

Was it this, self-love, self-loathing, which clocked the workings of the heart from the beginning?

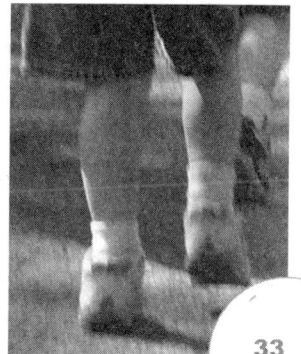

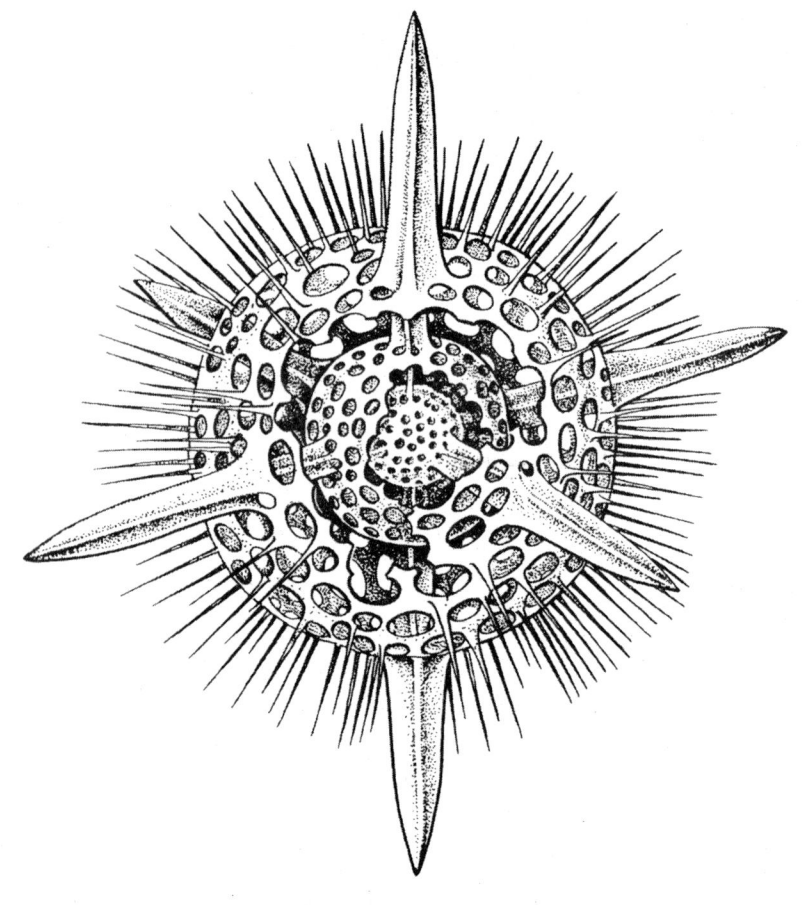

GLOBAL WARMING

After the initial weeks of sleep, and of forgetting, Noah and I took to phoning each other at frequent sporadic intervals. Sometimes several times a day, as though reporting mutual contractions to one another. *Contraction, release.* In turn, we were seized by sudden swimmings of the eyes, constrictions of the throat, spinnings in the head, convictions it would be best to play dead, there seemed no where else to go from here.

In turn, we were overcome by waves, set loose by something as small as the scalding of a pot of milk, or the loss down the drain of a silver chain. These overcomings seldom happened simultaneously, one of us always prepared to be present and heavy as an anchor. *Contraction, release.* Most often we'd both be dragged down, regardless who triggered the deluge. Regardless who had *again* been unable to resist the compulsion to *pick up the phone, push the buttons, hear the voice.*

I'm just calling to say hello, the more imperiled one would say, and the other one would say *Hello. How are you?* Then the first voice, the trembling one, would scarcely make it through the first note of *I'm fine,* when something would burst, behind the eyes, in the throat, the pit of the stomach. And the beloved would drown, right there, on the other end of the phone line, while the other could do nothing to save them anymore. *Rather throw myself at the wreck of this,* said Noah, *than watch it sink from the shore.*

Noah's cries sometimes came as a frightening chord, low and sustained, like the creaky opening of an old wooden door. A castle door, a barn door, or the door his namesake lowered onto dry earth, to let out all the animals. I was privately frightened by this, the initial part of his cry, the force of the hinge which it held back. Soon they would all come forth, the wounded birds and limping oxen, the elephants with patches over their eyes, all the sad inhabitants of our sad Ark. I would want to collect them to me in my arms, crossed over my own chest, rocking back and forth so slowly and dumbly, so tightly that the last drops of water are wrung from them.

Human Error. As though there were any other kinds. As a species, we are quite proud of our memory and foresight, but it is only in relation to these that the concept of *error* can be said to exist at all. Mistakes appear to be a human invention. Technical errors, or mechanical errors, or even acts of God which are thought to be unfortunate, are only erroneous according to human faculties of memory and foresight.

It's only relative to some sense of where you've *been* and where you want to *go,* that you can possibly go the wrong direction. Otherwise, you're just there, like a protozoa, always in the right place at the right time because there is no other possibility. *If you are to be preyed upon, so be it. You can't foresee it, so amen then.* If the will of God is unerring, perhaps it is also unconscious, like a protozoa.

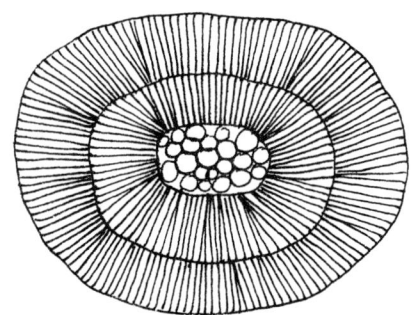

Noah used to have an old globe of the world which lit up when you plugged it in. It sat on a tree stump by our bed. I watched an illuminated insect jump suddenly northwest, from Poatowchen to Biisk, then down southwest to Khandahar.

A few hundred miles southwest of the Hawaiian Islands was a hole in the middle of the ocean. It was roughly the size and shape of Spain. I could stick my whole thumb through it, and feel the heat of the light bulb at the Earth's core. *Sixty watts.* Noah had kept telling me to remind him to change the bulb. He'd intended to take out the sixty watt bulb, and replace it with a forty watt. Because as it was, the centre was too hot, and was causing surface melt in certain locations. The names of the countries were turning brown and incinerating themselves, and the borders too. Noah asked me to remind him to fix this.

Every night I watched the meridians of longitude rust and widen, like iron weldings on the side of an old ship. *Would it fall apart in sections, then, like an overripe orange? Or would it melt on top, and cave in, like a jack-o-lantern?*

When I look at tombstones, I think of rotten teeth. Death is that point where we cease to ruminate upon the world, and gnash our teeth. Finally through consuming it, it consumes us. Not as a human consumes, in gobbles and slurps, and not like gnashing mechanical jaws. The earth eats like a bird. Constantly, and in small units, grinding us between the tiny and cumulate grains in its gizzard. The earth is a hen, it has no teeth, but finely it grinds us. It grounds us.

All pushing is pushing toward an end. All pulling is pulling toward an end. Like my father on his rickety rowing machine in the basement, *Pull, release. Pull, release.* He was stasis in motion in my mind. So I did *not* remind Noah to change the bulb at centre of the Earth, I did not. *How many would it take to change it?* I did not *remind* him, but *pulled* him down to the flood of the bed, and pushed the switch of the globe to *Off* with my thumb. *Pulling to a crisis. Pushing to a crisis. Release.*

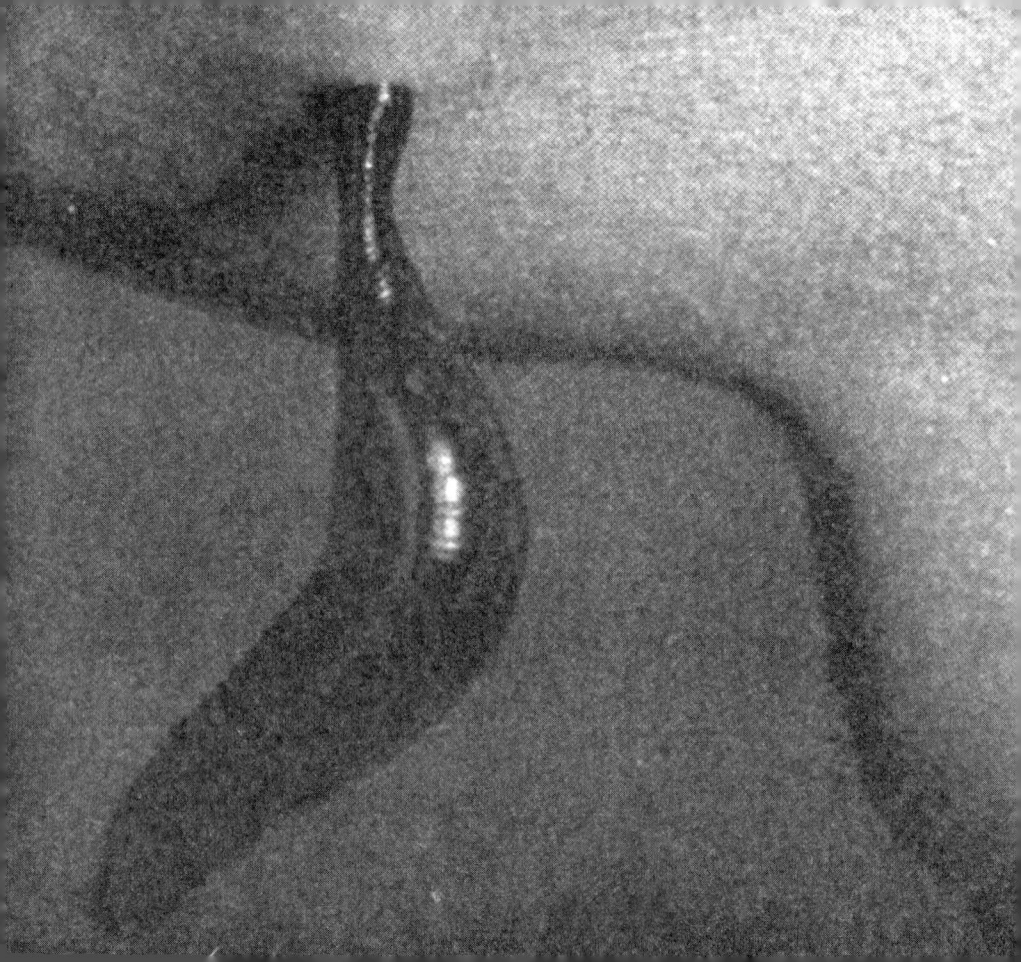

THE TALE OF THE HORSE-LEECH

A parable of insatiability, written for Agnes, on the occasion of her 11th birthday, by her father Luther Underhill

The horse-leech has two daughters,
Give & Give.
There are three things that will not be satisfied,
Four that will not say,
Enough:
Shoel, and the barren womb,
Earth that is never satisfied with water,
And fire that never says,
Enough.
The eye that mocks a father,
And scorns a mother,
The ravens of the valley will pick it out,
And the young eagles will eat it.

— Proverbs 30:15-17

Once upon a time at the bottom of a pond lived a leech of peculiar size. It had two fine suckers, one at each end of itself, with which it was able to move along the muddy floor like a slinky, endlessly, endoverendoverend. Just as certain flies of peculiar size were known as *horse-flies,* because they're as large as a *horse,* this leech was known as the *horse-leech* because it was large as a *house,* or had once been large as a house. But after several lean years in the absence of those to whom the leech could really feel *attached*, it had shrunk, to the size of a horse. The *U* was lost in the translation, as it were, and its absence soberly noted: *U was lost.*

Are lost, corrected a little girl named Agnes, who was hearing the story for the first time.

R was lost? queried the leech, slinking round her little finger, and attaching himself to a benign mole on the palm of her hand, which was a part of herself the girl knew very well, like the back of her hand. The girl also knew that sometimes her hands were so large she'd find stray horses grazing on the palms, or other times they shrank as small as a flea in the ear of the horse, and she'd have to speak gently to her hands, and listen carefully, to hear all they heard.

No, insisted Agnes, *R was not lost. You are lost.*

So then *U* became lost, and *R* took its place, and the leech shrank to the size of a *horse,* which was smaller than a *house,* but still quite large for a leech. The leech sadly took a stick and wrote a poem about himself, scraped wetly in the sand along the beach. Here is the poem.

The Horse Leech *by Luther Underhill*

When the leech reached his nadir of diminishing size,
He felt ashamed to have become so lost, in his daughter's eyes

So he sulkily slunk way down in the mud,
Til he'd sunk just as far as a leech could sink.
There, he felt things that all leeches feel in their blood,
Which primarily concerns finding something to drink.

Whenever sanguinary drinking-partners popped by for a chat,
The leech would drink them under the table, or on the doorstep welcome-mat.

He sucked up all the fishes, and the ducks and geeses too,
whose feet dangled like lures to his all-sucking view.
He sucked up the willows who wept on the bank,
like widows who weep for a ship that has sank.
He sucked up the bulrushes brushing the shore,
seduced a dozen swooping swallows in for tea.
He swallowed every swallow til there weren't any more,
And chortled at how mouthy he could be.

Any V-shaped flock of geese bound for destinations south,
Was rerouted with a road-sign to his great all-sucking mouth.
And though by his own estimation the leech's stature grew,
It conversely shrank in the eyes of others, of whom there now were few.

(I believe at this point there's one thing I should say
Regarding the sex of the leech, by the way:
Although up to this point we've been calling him 'he',
It is equally true that each leech is a 'she'.
For leeches, you know, possess parts of both types
In the folds of their annuli, which are their stripes.

Yet despite this, the leech, in its mud-bed embedded,
won't do well if to only itself it is wedded.
If its species is destined to stay in the game
It must find itself mirrored in those of the same —
as well as the opposite —
Sex. For clearly it's proven, when leeches are mated,
that sexes aren't opposite, just inversely placated.)

But that night in his mud-bed as the leech lay
Digesting the various events of the day,
Each creature grumbled in his belly
In whatever voice it knew
and each one told the leech its story,
Which was now his story, too.

"I'll hear your dreary tales if you must tell them," yawned the leech.
"But do omit the parts which suck, is all I would beseech.
And I hope you'll be so kind as not to curse me for your fate —
You'd've all had to go some time, I only helped firm up the date."

But the fish rebuked his theory that they'd someday have grown limbs,
they'd booked the next few million years to finish up their swims.
And though the swallows flirted with the earth, they'd no intention of embrace
since to swallows such a union would be death in any case.
And the willows only wept because it suited them to do so —
Their limbs drooped not out of sorrow, but because they simply grew so.

As for those who paddled on the water when not waddling on the land,
No screw loose in their bird-brains made them loath to take a stand
Upon one firmament over to the other. They swung both ways
because they had the proper gear to do it —
Given chance to try
both sea and sky,
Shouldn't one at least review it?

"But I suck," wailed the leech, "So what else can I do?
And sucking can scarcely be said to exist
In the same way that paddling does for a duck.
For a duck can fly south when long winters persist,
But if one is a leech, one needs something to suck.

If a willow needs no reason to weep,
What cruel design makes me so needy?
If a swallow loves, but does not take,
What divine mistake makes me so greedy?

The rump of a horse takes nothing from me
How came I then to so miserable a course?
By what unkind Divine or else Darwinian decree
Am I worse than a scourge on the arse of a horse?"

The leech buried himself in the cool dark mud
Then covered his ears, did the leech.
He stood like a man on the bridge of his fears
and split the night air with a screech...

"When I think of the life I've sucked away it makes my belly ache,
And I long to reverse the natural course which I've been forced to take.
The memory of willows makes but mournful company
When, aside from the mud at the bottom of this pond,
There is no one left but me."

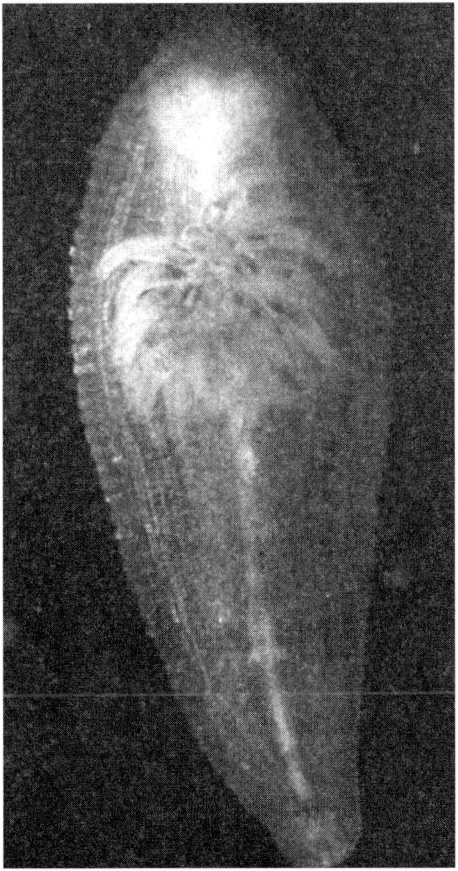

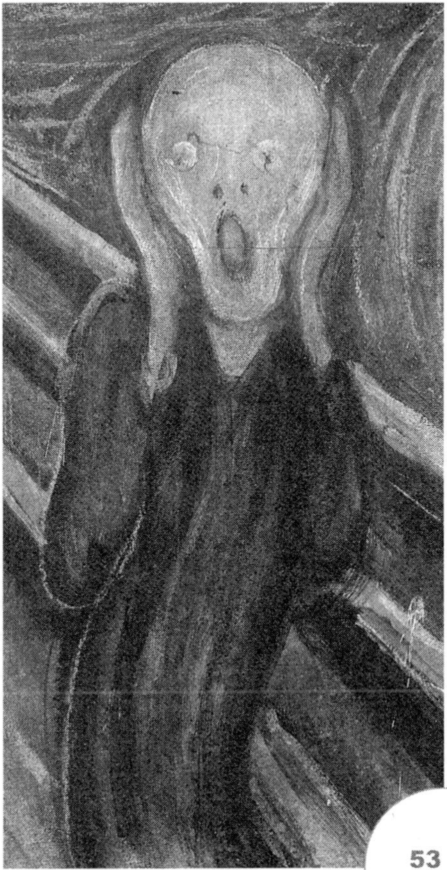

HAPPY,
THE 3-LEGGED GHOST-HAMSTER

Could we with ink the ocean fill
And were the sky of parchment made,
Were ev'ry stalk on earth a quill
And ev'ry man a scribe by trade,
To write the love of God above
Would drain the ocean dry,
Nor could the scroll contain the whole
Tho stretched from sky to sky.

— Rabbi Mayer, 1096 Germany
Written on the wall of the mental institution
wherein he died.

This is how the story goes. The squiggly lines in my mind, the ones my mother was certain were hysteria or something more sinister, gradually migrate like faraway geese heading south, down into my hands, where they perch and become restless. They slap their leather feet into the meat of my palms, and peck along the small bones of my fingers. I feel them ruffle and settle themselves. I see their footprints, and know them like the back of my hand, their webbed toes figured in bones on the back of my hand.

I become extraordinarily conscious of my hands. I wring them, wring out diapers with them, rub ointment into their knuckles, which are red and cracked like udders. I hold baby Rose and her stuffed giraffe in them, pace the floor, stop suddenly and weep for all and no reasons. I am seduced by a goose-down comforter, but seek out a mummified storage closet instead, and start hauling out boxes. The back of the closet is full of giant insects, spindly broom-bugs and bucket-beetles, and a machine which cleans carpets with its million legs, and a plastic cocoon to wrap up my mother's head until it is dried and set.

Finally I find it, the thing I didn't even know I was looking for. That large green beetle of a typewriter my father used to tap out his god-words on, his weird little parables about leeches and what all else. I pull the typewriter out of the closet, then have to reach back into the mustiness and feel around for one of its feet, which has broken off. It is very surprising to find my father's old typewriter here at my mother's new place. I don't understand why it's here, moldering in storage, instead of with my father. There comes a mute anger, that he'd be so pathetic as to leave his favourite thing behind. Similar to my mother's annoyance at him for adopting so many three-legged hamsters. We never heard the end of that.

Your father is one of those men who believes it's morally superior to have only three legs, even if you're supposed to have four, my mother would say. *He seems to think handicaps indicate depth of character.*

That hamster is not handicapped, my father would defend, *it is merely challenged.*

If a thing which is missing is exchanged for a thing which resembles it minutely, it is unlikely that most people will notice the switch. This was why my brother Gavin believed our parents were actually aliens, and why every hamster who ever lived at the house on Dormier street had only three legs. Because the first one had only three legs. But I always had to wonder how my father managed to get in touch with so many three-legged hamsters.

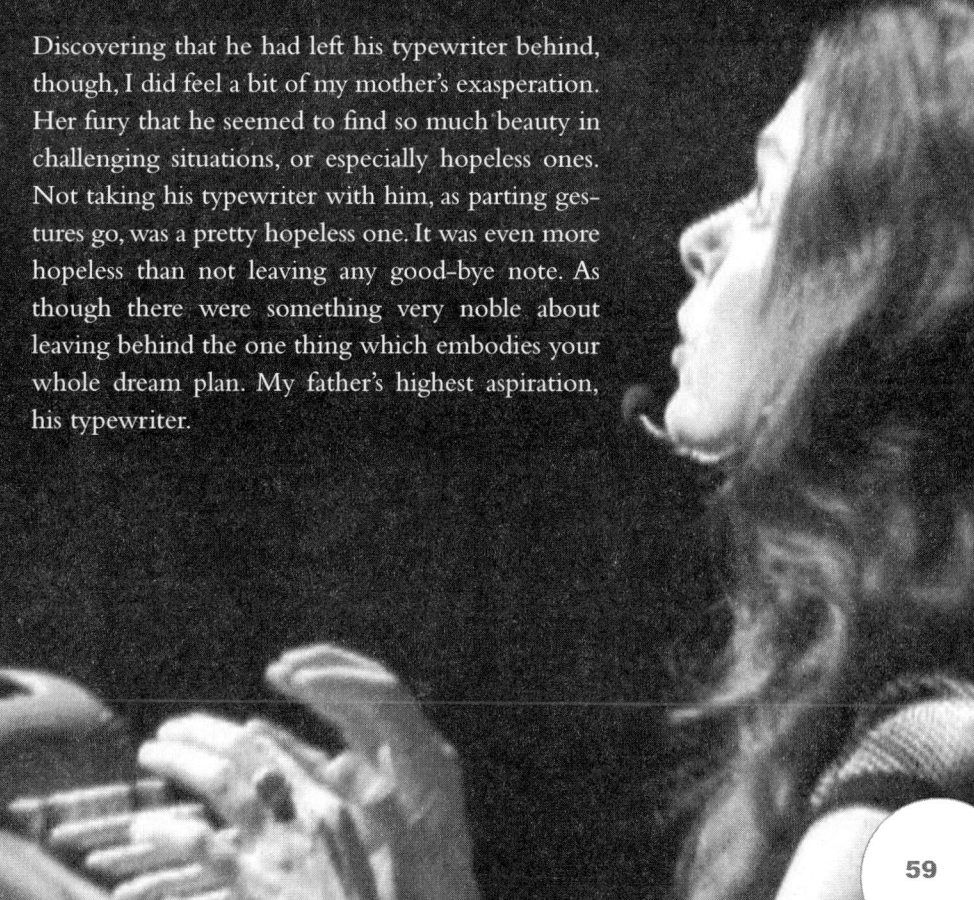

Discovering that he had left his typewriter behind, though, I did feel a bit of my mother's exasperation. Her fury that he seemed to find so much beauty in challenging situations, or especially hopeless ones. Not taking his typewriter with him, as parting gestures go, was a pretty hopeless one. It was even more hopeless than not leaving any good-bye note. As though there were something very noble about leaving behind the one thing which embodies your whole dream plan. My father's highest aspiration, his typewriter.

Still, I wouldn't have gone through the whole storage closet, looking for that spidery old machine, if I didn't half-expect to find it there. I wasn't sure whether this half-expectation were a form of disrespect, or a form of understanding. People's expectations can cause dizziness if they are too high, but they are crushing when they are too low. People's expectations can be like second hand snow suits, which don't fit you particularly well and are ugly, but sometimes you're forced to wear them anyhow.

On the other hand, my father's typewriter could only be here at Salmon Court, if my mother had taken the trouble to bring it with her during the move. Instead of liquidating it, with the rest of my father's leftover personal effects, when she sold the house on Dormier Street. I am a bit surprised she kept it. She never mentioned there being any typewriter at all, here at her place, obviously, since I was not to overstimulate my brain with things like words until I was quite quite well again.

But back to the original hand, I wouldn't have found the typewriter at all, if my mother hadn't for *some* reason decided to keep it. My father had abandoned it, deliberately or not, then my mother had preserved it, deliberately or not. So with some small deliberation it became compulsive to recycle it, the cumulate process calling in all other hands.

So I am learning to type, Rose. Hands have their own memory, and are hopeful. They reach, they hover over keys trying to remember, they find their pace and scuttle along with purpose until they hit another glitch. But I notice there are certain words which my hands insist on misspelling. *Mother,* whenever my hands try to type it, always comes out *mouther.* And *father,* when I have cause to write it, comes out *faither.*

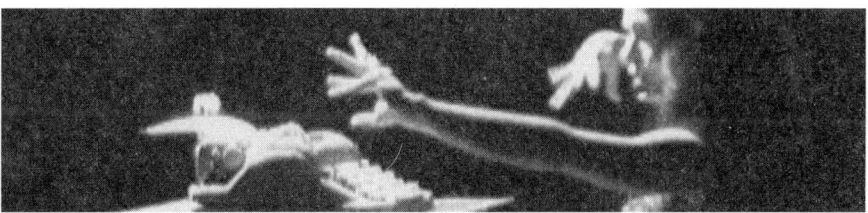

The typewriter ribbon is bichromatic, bisected bilaterally in two colours of ink. I turn the spindles upside down, and type in red, to see if this changes anything. Whether typing in red opens more direct channels to the heart of the matter.

Matter, fodder. I set up the typewriter on a yellow milk crate on the floor, in the *faith* that planting myself on the ground will help me connect with what everything is built upon, where everything finds its roots. I have to keep my *mouth* shut about reasonings like these, having learned that people don't so much care what private eccentricities you cultivate, but they *do* care if your reasons for cultivating them are too unironic.

My mother assumed, for instance, that the row of drying apple cores on my bedroom windowsill was *simple depressive messiness*, until I told her that I planned to collect three hundred of them and plant an orchard one day. Now the row of apple cores is like a pentagram on my door, and my mother suddenly develops superstitions about every living thing in the house. There are suddenly more mothballs than I've ever seen in the hall closet, and my daughter Rose has a fortified yellow net over her crib, so no cats will steal her soul through her mouth.

Mouther. Faither. Once it is warm, I move the milk crate outside, and behind the trees a bit, so my mother can't see me as I watch her sitting and coddling Rose, and breathing in my daughter's breath. The milk crate makes harlequino patterns on the grass. The froth of spit bugs, and the furred helmets of tall grasses brush my bare legs. My brother Gavin and I used to fight wars with those grasses, the ones whose heads could be struck off when you whipped them with another piece of same type of grass. It had been a bit of shock to be holding forth your bobbing head, then suddenly be struck and left holding only the stem. The heads had snapped off so cleanly, like asparagus.

Mother, mother. Father, father. O and I. Those are the extra letters, the ones my typing hands fill in as a joke on my two half-brains. *Faith,* the awareness that thoughts and activities participate in a pattern, perhaps even that meaning can be discovered, or invented, by paying attention to the pattern. *Faith,* like the rhythm of pulse, or the sound of my father rowing back and forth on his rickety rowing machine in the basement, *pull, release.*

Mouth, an aperture, a simian crease. A dragon's cave where stalactites and stalagmites grind themselves in sleep. The dragon-tongue lies coiled, licks fire, spits sparks. It plays with the place where a tooth is loose, the chink in armour. *Mouth,* the eventual gateway of utterance. *Faith,* the rhythm of pulse sustained.

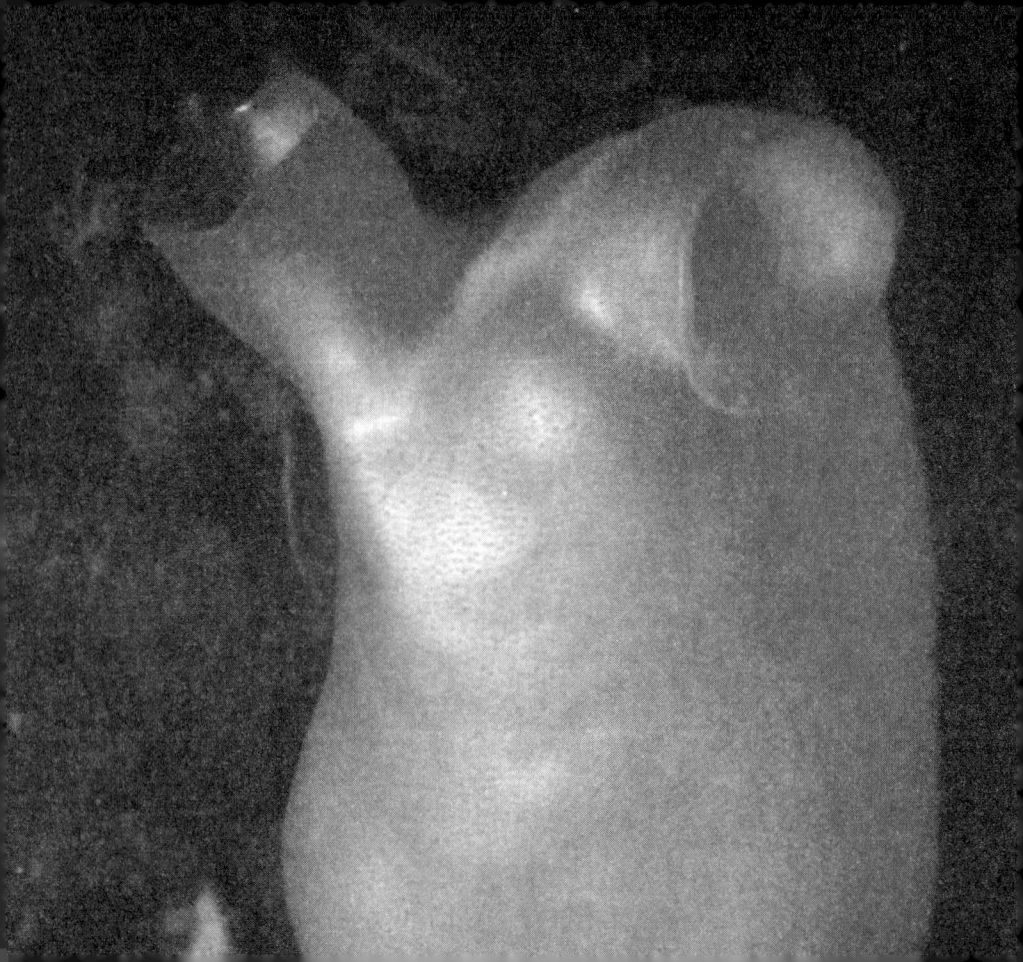

SEA PEACH

Love breathes underwater like sea creatures,
slow in how it teaches, gliding grazing like a graceful ray
an opening anemone, raising tendrils in time to the pulse of the sea
and drawing them in again. It's only enemy that toothy little fish anxiety
for years it followed me, nipping my Achilles from behind
to remind me of times I was blind to love that never left
when buried, bereft my heart burrowed low
so no one else could bruise it, didn't know
that hiding was the only way to lose it.

Since the Ice Age she'd been down
in the basement digging through boxes
trying to find something she thought she'd lost.
The original skin of shape-shifting foxes
the thing she swore not to lose at any cost.
She'd come to believe she was not a real person
maybe a creature someone put a curse on, assuming
human form and learn a lesson while she's here.
A shape-shifter, a drifter, more at home roaming
open fields alone, than tethered to another
and living under cover in a room no matter how warm.
She'd come to miss the furred perk of her alert ears,
the magic broomstick of her tail, her padded paws

turning circles thrice before she sleeps.
But whatever original skin she was born with is hidden away somewhere in a box
so no human lover would ever discover she's not actually a girl, but a fox.
One who walks and talks like a regular girl, but if she falls in love
its the end of the world, for her, the permanent transfer from one life
form to another. If love ever uncovered her original skin,
she might never fit back into it again, slip into it and slink out the door.
She might never be the same as she was before.

Then she met you and she wasn't afraid, though you didn't feel like a choice
she had made at first. More like a kind of emulsion or
expulsion from the secret garden of her discontent,
you must have been heaven sent. She'd prayed for answers from the sky but
looked to earth for her reply, the nodding god of *Yes* who was so welcome in your eye.
Your heart beat a happy tattoo so she opened the door and
yes it was true, nothing was the same as it had been before
you. Like shiny scales of goldfish you opened
eyes on her skin, and they wept out oceans lying within
old loves flood away to make room for a new one
didn't think she had it left in her to even pursue one
then recent questions as to whether she was even human.

And letters that she didn't send, loves she swore would never end
apology calls she didn't make, loves lost or tossed by blind mistake
and all the roads she didn't take. Love's the one who's hard to find
love's the one who knows your mind, love's the one who feeds your soul
love's the one to have and hold
But hold a minute, hold how?
There's a hundred hungry ways to hold her up or hold her down
will she still be able to get around? will she be able to hold her ground?

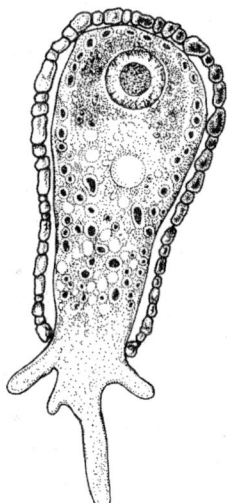

So she digs down deep to the bottom of the box
to find the original hide of the fox,
and it's there all right, despite
paranoia some lover would thieve it
slip it on and slink away.
The choice was always hers to retrieve it
but who wears furs these days?
perhaps her fears had fallen out of fashion
perhaps there were more human ways of nurturing a passion.

But look, beside the fox at the bottom of the box,
a book about biology. And being a student of life she took hold
of it in her own hands, she let it unfold
in hopes it would offer a lesson to teach.
It fell open to the name *Halocynthia auranthium*
or in more common terms, the *Sea Peach*.
The sea peach is a creature who looks like a heart
living at the bottom of the ocean
rooted in place by a sucker on its underpart
grounded, holding steady as devotion, its evolution
has chosen this sort of lifestyle.

Halocynthia auranthium
luminous hues of a peach chrysanthemum
by sublime chance or divine artistry
with two branching siphons raised overhead,
like the aorta and the pulmonary artery.
One to take things in, one to give things out
the sea peach teaches what the heart is about.
Through its two siphons the sea peach feeds,
breeds, and breathes, taking in food and oxygen,
inspiration, exhaling tiny tadpoles to the tide
to reroot themselves elsewhere, in some other place.
All this from a creature who has no face.
No crises of identity, the ability to simply be
no mind, but no matter, none of the clatter
and chatter of the human brain,
no broken-hearted sea peach ever drove itself insane
and its offers of asylum have no locks on either side.
So she chose the book of life, and closed the box on the fox-hide.

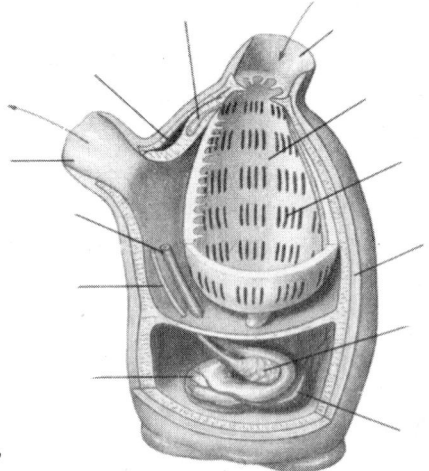

Phylum Chordata. The sea peach is a chordate just like me,
the marine iguana, great horned toad, and the chimpanzee.
Which means we all have spinal-structures just like you,
the giant squid, the gerbil, and the caribou.
Each who shares the chordate name starts out
looking pretty much the same, at least in our prenatal form
then we start to shift our shapes after we're born.
From guinea hens to wide mouth bass,
we all begin as tadpoles, with something like a head
and something like a tail. Headstrong and wriggling,
just like the rest of us, prairie chickens, gila monsters,
arctic perch and hippopotamus,
cheetahs, horses, salamanders, goats and stoats and geese and ganders,
and the sea peach, too, to name but a few.
We all begin with heads and tails
but it's here in evolution the sea peach derails
it doesn't grow a spine, and it doesn't grow a face
it only grows a sucker to ground itself in place
like a heart who hears the murmur
of its purpose here on earth, it finds a spot
of ocean floor and settles toward rebirth.

She studies the sea peach a very long time
til it seemed she'd almost become one
not in the sense of losing her spine,
but the sense of trusting in someone.
First comes a voice, then comes a choice.
Maybe it comes from within and ripples without,
and quietly it tells you what your life is about
in murmured whispers thumping somewhere in your chest.
Or it comes from without and touches within,
and opens up a million tiny eyes on your skin
and you can see clearly now.

Catherine Kidd is the author of two previous conundrum press publications: *everything I know about love I learned from taxidermy* and *psittacine flute*.

Jack Beetz is a DJ and music mastering engineer. In his studio, Chopstick, he cuts records and dub plates for artists in New York, Montreal and abroad.

ACKNOWLEDGEMENTS

These performance pieces are adapted from Kidd's novel *Bestial Rooms,* to be
   published by Thomas Allen. Thanks to Patrick Crean and Katja Pantzar.
Thanks to the Canada Council for the Arts and their Spoken and
   Electronic Word program.
Thanks to Sherwin Tjia for his preliminary design work.
Thanks to DNA Productions for their sound advice.

Cat and Jack wish to thank our mothers and fathers, Andy Brown, Ian
Ferrier, Antoine Mazet, Billy Mavreas, Tod Van Dyk, Joanne Hui, Casa
del Popolo, Paul Seesequasis, Corey Frost, Chez Vito [taxidermy rental],
Louis Rastelli [Distroboto], Studio Lyne St. Roch [yoga], Victoria
Stanton, Lewis Carroll, Eileen Garrett, Dr. Suess, Vincent Tinguely, Mike
Paterson, Caroline Ryser, Jeff Saffin [photo page 56], Edvard Munch
[*The Scream* on page 53], Sabrina Usher [bio photo], Concordia
University, Mike Burns, Katherine Gombay, CBC/Radio Canada,
Chai the cat, Jing Bong the dog, and God.

Illustrations on pages 18, 38, 52 by Joanne Hui.

Photographs on pages 20, 59, 61, 63 taken by Tod Van Dyk from video stills of a performance at Theatre Lachapelle.

Many of the animal and ameobic illustrations are by Turid Hölldobler and are taken from *Animal Architecture* by Karl von Frisch (1974) including the diagram of the exoskeleton of a single-celled radiolaria on page 34.

Photographs on pages 15, 16, 17, 30, 33, 66 by Andy Brown.

Illustrations on pages 10 and 11 by Billy Mavreas.

The Holstein cow-tub pictured on pages 26 and 39 went missing from Catherine's balcony. We assume it flew away. But if you see a one-legged cow-tub, please return it to Catherine, who has the other three feet.

Please note that the furry blur on page 42 is a red fox spotted in the Montreal Cemetery.

Sea peach and other pictures taken from *Biology*, Raven & Johnson, 3rd edition.

Words and Voice: Catherine Kidd
CD mixed, arranged and produced by Jack Beetz
Executive producer for Wired on Words: Ian Ferrier
www.wiredonwords.com / poets@wiredonwords.com

1. Downward Facing Dog

2. A Big Fat Hen

3. The Walking Man

4. Global Warming

5. The Tale of the Horse Leech

6. Happy the 3-Legged Ghost Hamster

7. Sea Peach

WOWCD06